Militarism
and
The Quality of Life

Alex C. Michalos

Canadian Papers in Peace Studies

1989 Number 1

Science for Peace/ Samuel Stevens
Toronto
1989

Samuel Stevens & Company
University of Toronto Press
5201 Dufferin Street
Downsview, Canada M5H 5T6

Science for Peace
University College
University of Toronto
Toronto, Canada M5S 1A7

Canadian Cataloguing in Publication Data

Michalos, Alex C.
Militarism and the quality of life
(Canadian papers in peace studies; 1989 no. 1)
Includes bibliographical references.
ISBN 0-88866-632-2

1. Militarism - Canada. 2. Militarism -
Influence. 3. Munitions - Canada. I. Science
for Peace (Association). II. Title. III. Series.

UA600.M52 1989   355'.0213   C89-094880-1

Contents

Preface

Science for Peace gratefully acknowledges the financial support of the Canadian Institute of International Peace and Security, the Pugwash Park Commission, and several generous personal donations toward the publication of the Canadian Papers in Peace Studies.

Papers submitted to the Publications Committee of Science for Peace for this series are each considered on their merits, having due regard to the purposes of Science for Peace. In addition, the Committee seeks authors for papers on topics that are thought to be of special importance at the time. The Committee has a general policy of submitting papers to independent referees for comment, but is not rigidly bound by this policy, and also seeks to avoid long delays when material of timely relevance is submitted.

Derek Paul, editor
Physics Department
University of Toronto
Toronto, M5S 1A7

Acknowledgements

An earlier version of this essay was presented at the University of Guelph, at a meeting of Science for Peace, May 24, 1988. Another version was written for a Conference on Ethical Issues in Military Research, originally planned for May 1988 but postponed to January 1989, co-sponsored by the Philosophy and Technology Studies Center of Polytechnic University of New York and the New York Academy of Sciences. I would like to thank the following people for helping me improve the final product: R.G. Good, B. Graf, L. Groake, R.R. Iyer, J. McMurtry, G. Morgan, C. Mitcham, S.S. Nagel, D.C. Poff, J.P. Roos and J.T. Stevenson.

Militarism and the Quality of Life

Alex C. Michalos

I

Introduction

In 1978 the United Nations General Assembly endorsed the Final Document of the first Special Session on Disarmament calling for the commission of a group of governmental experts to examine the relationships between disarmament and development. Twenty-seven experts were selected from every continent, with Inga Thorsson designated as Chairperson. The Group's official Report was submitted to the UN Secretary-General in October 1981. The Report included nine Recommendations, and this essay is a relatively limited attempt to respond to the following two:

"The Group recommends that all governments, but particularly those of the major military powers, should prepare assessments of the nature and magnitude of the short- and long-term economic and social costs attributable to their military preparations, so that the general public can be informed of them. ...

1

"The Group recommends that governments urgently undertake studies to identify and to publicise the benefits that would be derived from the reallocation of military resources in a balanced and verifiable manner, to address economic and social problems at the national level, and to contribute towards reducing the gap in income that currently divides the industrialised nations from the developing world and establishing a new international economic order." (Sanger 1982, p.107).

In the next section (II) I present an overview of some social indicators for Canada and the United States covering the years from about 1963 to 1983. Following this, I review Canadian federal government expenditures in general for the period from 1974 to 1986 (section III). Section IV summarizes available information on the Canadian arms industry, including production and export figures. In section V I present 15 arguments against the Canadian production and export of military arms broadly construed. After that I consider 16 arguments in favour of the production and export of arms, and offer critical replies to each of them (section VI). Insofar as my arguments are sound, a case should have been made for resisting the current federal government's proposed increases in the production and export of arms, and for beginning to scale down current militaristic activities.

II

An Overview for Canada
and the United States of America

Some of the groundwork for the present investigation was prepared in my North American Social Report (five volumes, 1980-2). In that work I compared the quality of life of Canadians and Americans in the 1964-74 period in the areas of population structure; mortality, morbidity and health care; criminal justice; politics; science and technology; education; recreation; natural environment and resources; transportation; communication; housing; economics; religion; morality and social customs. Broadly speaking, three conclusions were reached. First: "On the basis of an examination of over 135 social indicators and over 1659 indicator values, it seems fair to say that the quality of life in the 1964-74 period was comparatively or relatively higher in Canada than in the United States." Second: "If one looks at the first and last recorded stock values for the usable indicators for each country independently of the other country, [one finds that] ... both countries improved in more ways than they deteriorated." Third, considering the responses of national probability samples of Canadians and Americans to over 117 Gallup-Poll questions: "The countries were more similar in the 1963-8 period than in the 1969-75 period." In short: "Taking the results of my analyses of nonindependent paths [social indicator trends] and opinion poll responses together, it seems fair to say that the countries tended to be or become dissimilar in more ways than they tended to be or become similar." (Michalos 1982, pp.171-4). Regarding

3

the specific item of military expenditures, "In the 1965-74 period American military expenditures as a percent of GNP were always two to four times higher than their Canadian counterparts ... In the final year the American figure stood at 6% of the GNP, compared to 2% for Canada." (Michalos 1980, p.176).

Although I planned to update all my numbers to 1984 and later, other projects always got in the way. However, Table 1 summarizes the results of comparing the rank-order values of Canada and the United States among 142 countries on 13 indicators for 1984, based on Sivard (1987). [Plus signs (+) in Table 1 designate positive indicators and minus signs (−) designate negative indicators].

Canada's rank-orders were preferable to those of the United States on 9 of the 13 indicators. According to Sivard's aggregation procedures, Canada was better off than the United States in "socio-economic standing" generally and in military expenditures. These are the most recent figures available, and I suppose the assessments would not have changed much by today. Assuming that government expenditures for social and economic purposes contribute more to a good quality of life than government expenditures for military purposes, the numbers in Table 1 suggest that Canadians have been able to make a more favourable trade-off on this score than Americans.

Table 1

Ranking Canada and USA among 142 countries on military and social indicators, 1984

Indicator	Canada	USA
Military:		
Expenditures per capita (–)	22	8
Expenditures per soldier (–)	6	4
Expenditures per square km (–)	89	24
Average social economic standing (+)	3	4
GNP per capita (+)	10	6
Education:		
Public expenditures per capita (+)	3	7
School-age population per teacher (+)	7	20
Percent school-age population in school (+)	3	6
Percent women in university enrolment (+)	13	16
Literacy rate (+)	5	5
Health:		
Public expenditures per capita (+)	6	8
Population per physician (–)	24	22
Infant mortality rate (–)	9	18
Life expectancy (+)	4	8
Nutrition:		
Calorie supply per capita (+)	17	5
Calories as percent of requirements (+)	26	10
Percent of population having safe water (+)	1	1
Number of preferable rankings*		
Negative	4	1
Positive	5	3
Total	9	4

* excluding the indicator for average socio-economic standing, and two indicators with tie scores.

Source: R.L.Sivard, World Military and Social Expenditures 1987 (World Priorities Inc., Box 25140, Washington, D.C. 20007) pp.46-7, Table 3. Sivard's text gives specific definitions of indicators and their sources.

III

Canadian Federal Government Expenditures

Table 2 lists the Canadian Federal government's total and defence expenditures for the 1974-88 period in millions of current Canadian dollars.

In the final year defence expenditures were estimated to be nearly $11 billion or 9% of total government expenditures. There has been a steady increase in defence expenditures as a percent of total expenditures since the 1984 federal election of a Progressive Conservative government. The 1987 figure is a bit above the 15 year average of 8.7%. However, according to the Tories' White Paper on defence policy, 'Challenge and Commitment: A Defence Policy for Canada' (Canada, Department of National Defence 1987, p.67): "The Government is committed to a base rate of annual real growth in the defence budget of two per cent per year after inflation, for the [coming] fifteen-year planning period." At the same time: "After 1986-7, the budget states that operating costs in all federal departments will not be permitted to rise by more than 2 percent in nominal terms each year, which, after inflation, is a real cut of 2 percent." (Prince 1986, p.39). If the defence budget does increase at the projected rate, then in 10 years it will be about 10.5% of total Federal government expenditures, which would be roughly its 1972 rate. Putting the 2% real growth rate for defence spending together with the 2% real cut rate for all other federal departments, by 1998 the defence budget would be about 12.5% of the total, or roughly what it was in 1970 (Tredenick 1984, p.21).

Table 2

Federal Government and Defence Expenditures
(current millions)

Year ended March 31	—Expenditures— 1 Total	—Expenditures— 2 Defence	Column 2/1 (%)
74	22,839	2,232	9.8
75	29,245	2,512	8.6
76	33,978	2,974	8.8
77	39,011	3,371	8.6
78	42,882	3,771	8.8
79	46,539	4,108	8.8
80	50,416	4,391	8.7
81	58,066	5,077	8.7
82	67,674	6,028	8.9
83	88,521	6,938	7.8
84	96,610	7,843	8.1
85	109,215	8,762	8.0
86	111,227	9,094	8.2
87	116,389	9,993	9.0
88	125,535	10,769	9.0

Sources:

Public Accounts of Canada 1988, 1986, 1982, 1978.

Table 3

first part

Federal Government Expenditures by Function
(percentages)

Yr ended Mar. 31	1	2	3	4	5	6	7	8	9
74	8.8	5.7	7.3	8.0	1.1	12.5	8.9	4.1	3.4
75	7.4	5.5	7.1	7.4	1.3	11.1	8.1	5.9	3.1
76	7.2	5.1	6.7	7.5	1.6	10.7	9.0	5.3	4.0
77	7.8	5.6	6.7	8.0	2.0	10.5	8.9	4.8	4.7
78	7.9	5.6	6.4	6.8	2.3	10.6	9.5	4.6	4.0
79	8.1	5.5	6.5	7.6	2.6	10.1	9.3	4.1	3.9
80	7.7	5.1	5.7	7.3	2.9	11.1	7.2	3.0	3.4
81	7.3	5.1	6.3	6.5	3.1	10.9	7.0	2.7	3.3
82	7.4	5.1	5.2	6.0	3.2	10.8	7.0	2.6	3.3
83	7.2	4.7	3.0	5.0	3.3	10.4	10.8	2.4	3.5
84	7.6	4.8	3.1	6.1	3.6	10.2	9.9	2.3	4.1
85	7.5	4.7	3.3	6.3	3.8	10.0	9.1	2.1	4.0
86	7.4	4.8	3.0	6.1	4.2	10.7	8.9	2.2	3.9

Column codes

1 National Defence   2 General
3 Transport and Communication   4 Health
5 Canada Pension Plan   6 Old Age Security
7 Unemployment Insurance   8 Family Allowance
9 Assitance to Disabled

Sources: Statistics Can., Federal Government Finances 1985 (68-211) pp.41-2, Table 8; 1982 pp.40-1, T12; 1979 pp.40-1, T14; 1976 pp.44-5, T16.

8

Table 3

continued

Federal Government Expenditures by Function
(percentages)

Yr ended Mar. 31	10	11	12	13	14	15	16	17	18
74	3.8	1.0	0.6	1.8	1.2	7.8	1.5	7.1	15.4
75	3.3	0.9	0.7	1.9	1.1	8.7	1.6	7.4	17.5
76	3.2	0.8	0.9	2.0	1.4	7.3	1.4	7.7	18.2
77	3.3	0.7	1.2	1.9	1.0	8.3	1.4	7.1	16.1
78	4.2	0.7	1.1	2.4	1.6	7.6	1.5	7.7	15.5
79	4.4	0.8	1.3	1.9	1.4	6.7	1.5	9.3	15.0
80	4.2	0.6	1.4	1.8	1.6	7.2	1.7	10.1	18.0
81	3.7	0.5	1.5	1.6	1.6	6.5	2.1	10.8	19.5
82	3.4	0.4	1.4	1.6	1.4	6.7	1.9	14.2	18.4
83	3.1	0.5	1.9	1.7	1.2	6.7	3.1	13.3	18.2
84	3.5	0.5	1.6	1.7	1.2	6.4	3.1	12.9	17.4
85	3.4	0.4	1.8	1.8	1.0	6.0	2.5	14.7	17.7
86	3.4	0.4	1.3	1.8	0.9	5.8	2.8	17.0	15.4

Column codes

10 Education

11 Environment

12 Housing

13 Foreign Aid and Affairs

14 Research Establishments

15 Transfers to other levels of Government

16 Transfers to its Own Enterprises

17 Debt Charges

18 All Other Expenditures

Sources: as for table 3, first part.

Table 3 puts defence shares of the total federal government expenditures in the context of the shares of 16 other functional areas and a residual 'others'.

Because Statistics Canada's accounting procedures are not exactly the same as those of the Federal government, there is roughly a percentage point difference between the figures published by the two agencies. On average, for example, the defence share according to Statistics Canada was about 7.6% rather than 8.7%. The Statistics Canada figures are preferable for present purposes because the 16 functional areas are more detailed and easier to identify than their counterparts in successive Federal Budgets.

Inspection of the figures in Table 3 shows that the defence share of the total expenditures is typically greater than 13 of the 16 substantive functional areas. Only Old Age Security payments, Unemployment Insurance payments and national debt charges tend to take bigger slices of the total pie. While the shares of Old Age Security and Unemployment Insurance payments typically run from one to three percentage points above the defence share, the national debt share tends to run about twice as high as that of defence. At a minimum what these figures suggest is that Canada's defence expenditures constitute a significant share of the total Federal government expenditures and raise provocative questions regarding the actual versus a more desirable distribution. Since most of this paper consists of specific arguments for less spending on the production and export of military arms broadly construed and of replies to arguments for more spending on such things, much more will be said about diverse trade-offs as our discussion proceeds.

IV

The Canadian Arms Industry

Since there is no generally accepted definition of 'military arms' broadly or narrowly construed, there is bound to be some controversy about any alleged measured level of production or export of such things. The estimates given here are taken mainly from Treddenick (1987) and Regehr (1987). According to Treddenick (1987, p.24), "the defence industrial base is that part of the nation's economy providing goods and services required to support military activities." Granting that the definition is very broad, it becomes more useful when it is operationalized by identifying "the defence industrial base in terms of current demands placed on Canadian industry resulting from expenditures for domestic defence procurement and for exports." The latter account comes very close to Regehr's (1987, p.212) when he writes: "For purposes of implementing control measures, the Canadian government should define a military commodity as a commodity purchased by a military force or agency." Presumably, both authors would exclude some items like food and housing supplies, and both would include not only weapons but "the support facilities and equipment that make weapons usable." (Regehr 1987, p.70; Treddenick 1986, pp.35-6). Treddenick specifies a "narrow industrial base" within the broader sector, which includes "industries producing specialized military equipment". Operationally, the narrow industrial base includes manufacturers of aircraft and parts, motor vehicles, shipbuilding, communications equipment and some chemicals insofar as the products are sold to military agencies. Applying these rough definitions and some appropriate caveats, he reaches the following conclusions:

"If economic significance means the amount of economic activity generated in the defence industries, then by comparison to total economic activity in Canada, the defence industrial base must be judged to be insignificant. Total defence production accounts for considerably less than one per cent of both gross domestic product and total employment. When the narrow defence industrial base alone is considered, these contributions fall to about one-third of a percentage point in each case. Defence production is also not significant in any single provincial economy. Only in Nova Scotia and New Brunswick does employment generated by defence production approximate one per cent of total provincial employment, in most provinces it is considerably less. Defence production must also be considered insignificant in terms of international trade. Defence exports, net of re-exports, currently account for less than one per cent of total merchandise exports while defence imports, including indirect imports, account for just over two per cent of total merchandise imports. Finally, because of its comparatively low level and because it is difficult to make a theoretical case for its transferability to the civilian sector, defence research and development must also be considered insignificant relative to overall economic activity. ... The relatively small size of the Canadian defence industrial base makes it extremely difficult to see it as the mainstay of the capitalist system in Canada, in either the Marxian or the Galbraithian sense." (Treddenick 1987, pp.50-1).

Table 4 and Fig. 1 provide a longer and more detailed view of Canadian military exports since 1959. The bottom line of Table 4 shows that about 73% of our exports have gone to the United States, 14.6% to

Europe and 12% to other places, mainly in the Third World.

While we have just seen that Treddenick would be one of the last people to exaggerate the economic significance of the Canadian arms industry, he remarks that "Not only have total exports consistently exceeded domestic demand by large amounts, but exports to the United States alone have done so. ... This export dependence of the defence industries, and particularly the dependence on a single country, is the outstanding economic feature of the Canadian defence industrial base." (Treddenick 1987, p.31).

Table 4

Canadian Military Exports 1959-86
(current millions — percentages are in parentheses)

———— Destination ————

Years	USA	Europe	Other	Total
1959-69	2,419 (79)	440 (14)	207 (7)	3,066
70	226 (67)	41 (12)	69 (20)	336
71	216 (64)	67 (20)	53 (16)	336
72	175 (58)	74 (24)	52 (17)	300
73	199 (64)	73 (23)	38 (12)	309
74	150 (54)	46 (16)	85 (30)	281
75	188 (67)	59 (21)	34 (12)	281
76	191 (57)	113 (34)	32 (9)	336
77	314 (57)	76 (14)	164 (30)	554
78	267 (55)	130 (27)	88 (18)	484
79	368 (65)	146 (26)	55 (10)	568
80	482 (67)	142 (20)	98 (14)	722
81	827 (72)	149 (13)	175 (15)	1,151
82	1,028 (72)	158 (11)	248 (17)	1,434
83	1,207 (81)	129 (9)	145 (10)	1,481
84	1,360 (78)	243 (14)	150 (8)	1,753
85	1,644 (86)	154 (8)	104 (5)	1,902
86	947 (68)	196 (14)	245 (18)	1,388
Total	12,209 (73)	2,434 (15)	2,040 (12)	16,684

Sources: E. Regehr, Arms Canada James Lorimer and Co., Toronto 1987) p.17, Table 2; K. Epps, 'Canadian Military Industry Update' in The Ploughshares Monitor No.8 (1987) p.12.

CANADIAN MILITARY TRADE WORLD-WIDE

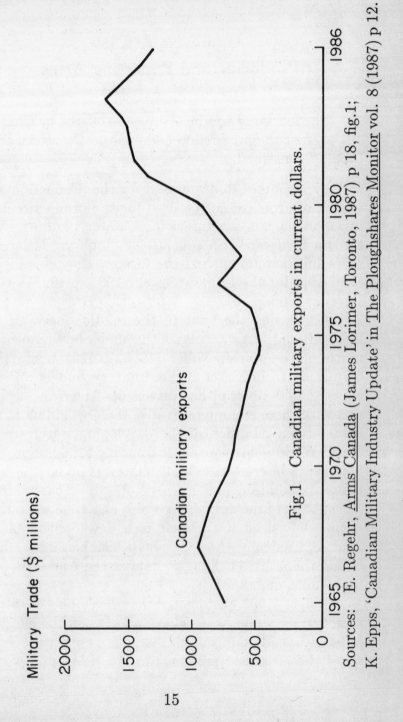

Fig.1 Canadian military exports in current dollars.

Sources: E. Regehr, Arms Canada (James Lorimer, Toronto, 1987) p 18, fig.1;
K. Epps, 'Canadian Military Industry Update' in The Ploughshares Monitor vol. 8 (1987) p 12.

V

Arguments against
Producing and Exporting Arms

The following arguments may be offered by Canadians against the production and export of military arms broadly construed.

1. Any resources that are used for the production and export of arms cannot be used for the production and export of such necessities as food, water, clothing, shelter, medical care and education. Since the latter are more life sustaining than the former, they should not be traded for the former (Regehr 1987, p.12; Wallace-Deering 1986, p.78).

Addressing the issue of the relation between the international arms race and the underdevelopment of much of the world, Miller (1986, p.126) wrote that "By massive increases in his military budget, [President Ronald Reagan] has driven up American deficits and with them real interest rates, thereby adding to the debt-servicing burden of the developing world. With Third World debts now approximating $900 billion, any increase in interest rates adds billions of dollars to these debts. In addition, high interest rates drain capital from the nations of the developing world at a time when they desperately need it for their own development plans. And so, ironically, those nations which can least afford it find themselves helping to finance the American military build-up."

Sanger (1982, p.46) noted that developing countries "are doubly vulnerable. They suffer when the effect of military spending in the industrialised countries aggravates the economic problems in the developed world, because they can then expect a slower flow of development aid, investment capital and technological know-how, as well as less quickly expanding markets for their exports. ... And the developing countries suffer also when their own military expenditures affect plans for their economic and social expansion." Additional corroborative details regarding the relation between the arms race and underdevelopment may be found in the Thorsson Report (1981); United Nations, Panel (1986); Perry (1986); Sivard (1986) and Gumbleton (1986).

2. Even if one ignores issues related to the export of arms, any resources that are used for the production of arms to be deployed by Canadian forces cannot be used for such necessities as food, clothing, shelter, medical care, education and other social services. According to Werlin (1986, pp.96-7), since the Mulroney government came to office in 1984, "Transfer payments from Ottawa to the provinces for health care and education have been reduced, unemployment insurance benefits have been cut back, public housing subsidies, environmental protection programs, and support for cultural activities (most importantly the Canadian Broadcasting Corporation) have all been reduced. Increases in the defence budget [averaging 6% a year for the rest of the decade] have quite simply been made by reducing the budget for public services." Thus, in the interest of promoting life sustaining programs and expenditures, increases in the production of arms should at least be kept below increases in other government programs and expenditures.

3. The availability of arms increases the inclination to resort to and the ability to use violent means to make social and political changes, and decreases the inclination to resort to and the ability to use non-violent means.

Again, since the latter are more life sustaining, they should be given priority over the former (Regehr 1987, pp.xvii, 194-5).

Adeniji (1987, p.105) made the connections quite clear in the following passage. "There have been more than 150 wars since 1945 fought in the developing countries, resulting in more deaths than in the Second World War. The number of countries that have been involved in these wars — about 80 — is an indication of disarray in the present security system as far as the third world is concerned. Internal conflicts caused by the neglect of the non-military aspects of security, regional distrust arising from territorial claims and other political factors are inflamed by the ready availability of arms for cash or in return for ideological solidarity. ... Through arms supplies, ideological battles are introduced into otherwise purely local disputes and solutions are rendered difficult."

Wilson (1986, pp.140-4) touched another aspect of the problem when she wrote that "The massive allocation of human and material resources to military research and development (fifty percent of all natural scientists work directly or indirectly for military purposes) has distorted the developed world's perception of what is socially useful and necessary. ... [and] ... International institutions, because of our inability to renew or reform them, have been paralyzed by the military build-up and lack of trust between countries."

Epps (1987, pp.8-9) reports on increases in Canadian National Defence contracts to university-based researchers under the Mulroney government. In Epps (1987a, p.10), former Defence Minister Perrin Beatty is quoted as saying that "The Department of National Defence has seen steadily increasing funds for research and development-directed contracts in Canadian industry. ... In the last ten years the expansion has been almost sevenfold."

4. Because Canada's biggest trading partner is the United States and about half of our manufacturing industry (not merely our arms industry) consists of American subsidiaries, much of our production and export is designed to American specifications, requirements and interests. Thus, much of what our arms industry produces and exports is designed to satisfy demands resulting from an American cold war vision of international Soviet threats to peace. Insofar as this is a biased vision and relatively dangerous for the continued existence of life on the planet, it would be wise to reduce all activities based on this vision, including all activities related to the production and export of arms (Regehr 1987, pp.xix, 53, 178, 181-2; DeRoo 1986, pp.84-7).

Galbraith (1986, p.107) provocatively and succinctly gave the following account of the origin and nature of the cold war bias. "The Soviet Union is indispensable to the American military power. Fear of the Soviet Union and tension in our relations directly and overtly serve our military power; any relaxation of tension would damage the resources it commands. From this comes the great fact of our time; tension is actually cultivated to support the military power. ... And in a world where military intelligence and enemy intention are extensively in the hands of the military, it would be astonishing were they not made to serve that tension. We accept this fact extensively — and, at budget time, very visibly. ... The concept of one superpower's relentless will to dominate the world serves the military designs of the other superpower. The hard fact of universal retreat must be kept subordinate to that need." Pentz (1986, p.276) takes a similar line.

5. In order to increase Canada's "capacity to assess and pursue independent and innovative foreign policy and defence options", we ought to decrease opportunities for the United States to influence our decision-making processes. Reductions in the integration of Canadian and American arms industries would significantly decrease such opportunities and they should therefore be undertaken (Regehr 1987, pp.xx, 29, 30, 179, 185; DeRoo 1986, p.86; Werlin 1986, p.101). According to Treddenick (1986, pp.38-9), "To confirm that military expenditures have an opportunity cost is not an argument against them; nor is the discovery that this opportunity cost is very high. Cost is only one-half of the equation, and probably the less important half. ... The other half of the equation must come to grips with the much more intractable problem of determining how a nation's preferences for military security are formed — how it perceives threats to its interests and how it sees its own particular role in the world."

6. Because Canada and the United States agreed to have a rough balance of arms trade through the 1963 Defence Production Sharing Arrangements (DPSA), Canada cannot expect long run economic gains from arms trade with the United States. Continued increases in the production and export of arms must rely on overseas markets. Because Europeans tend to insist on exchanges similar to those of the DPSA, the most promising markets are those of the Third World. However, if we increase sales of arms to Third World countries then we will also increase the carnage of wars, economic dependence and distorted social development. It has been estimated that as many as 20 million people have died in the 150 wars mentioned earlier (Regehr

1987, p.11). Besides contributing to the massacre, increases in the importation of weapons create foreign exchange shortages that relatively poor countries try to alleviate through greater exploitation of their natural resources for export. Thus, they develop dependent subsidiary economies incapable of indigenous innovation that might allow them economic independence in the long run. Distorted economies then, contribute directly to distorted social development, since the greatest burden of government expenditures must be devoted to international debt services rather than to social services (Regehr 1987, pp.12, 173-4). In many ways, as Regehr explains, if Canadians increase their traffic in arms to Third World countries, we will inevitably reproduce some of the debilitating effects on them that trade with the United States has on us (For a more detailed analysis of this point see Michalos 1982, pp.58-63).

7. Increases in the production and export of arms to Third World countries would increase the militarization of those countries, not only by increasing the amount of military hardware at their disposal but by encouraging any tendencies they might have toward authoritative and centralized political decision-making (Sivard 1986, p.25). "The military," Regehr (1987, p.14) writes, "... represents ... an ... organizational structure, with a high degree of centralization and hierarchy. The emphasis is on command and subordination, on discipline rather than creativity, with alternative thinking and approaches frequently defined as 'subversive'." Since increases in the militarization of Third World countries tend to undermine their democratic institutions and participative decision-making, such increases ought to be resisted. As Kelly (1986, p.221) wrote, "Both our

21

struggle against the arms race, and our struggle for human rights in all parts of the world must be fought simultaneously. ... It is wrong to say that human rights must be a condition for disarmament; and it is wrong to say that human rights will be the consequence of disarmament. Both must take place together, as part of a single process, the making of a democratic peace — a peace that will not be oppressive."

8. Increases in the production and export of arms will tend to increase the number of people in Canada whose livelihoods depend on militarization. Moreover, it is likely that most (certainly not all) people whose livelihoods depend on militarization will be relatively uncritical of militarization. Since militarization is inconsistent with our democratic institutions, inclinations and practices, the latter would be undermined by increases in the production and export of arms. Hence, increases in the production and export of arms ought to be resisted in the interest of protecting our own democratic institutions, inclinations and practices.

9. Because the arms industry tends to be highly specialized and concentrated, labour and material costs tend to be relatively high. As indicated in my reply to argument #11 below, the arms industry tends to be characterized by relatively low productivity. The combination of these characteristics implies that increases in arms production have inflationary effects as costs outrun productivity gains. Werlin (1986, p.98) notes that arms production is inflationary because it generates "spendable income without at the same time enlarging the supply of goods available in the market place." Hence, in the interest of reducing inflation, increases in the production and export of arms ought to be resisted (Melman

1984, pp.2-3; Sanger 1982, pp.41-3, 73-4; Regehr 1987, pp.164-5).

10. It has been estimated that if one percent of the over 50,000 nuclear weapons currently stockpiled by the USA and the USSR were exploded, there would be a nuclear winter of from six months to three years which most people on the planet could not survive. Since increases in the production and export of arms raise the likelihood of wars and, since any wars could accidentally initiate a global nuclear war leading to a nuclear winter, increases in the production and export of arms ought to be resisted (Pentz 1986, p.275, 291).

In the discussion after the presentation of his paper at the 1986 Vancouver Symposium, Pentz (1986, p.301) said he would make the following "... list of possible scenarios for the privilege of unleashing Armageddon. First on my list is that one side would incorrectly perceive the other side's intentions and capabilities. We are in a chronically dangerous situation at present, because both sides constantly apply, or misapply, worst-case analysis. ... The second most likely cause of nuclear war is an accident ... of the kind involving a simple failure of systems. ... Murphy's Law likes complex systems. The third most likely cause is an unpremeditated escalation of a small, local conflict. The fourth cause — which I don't believe can be eliminated — is madness in high places." Similar lists of possibilities may be found in Garcia-Robles (1987, p.86) and El-Shafei (1987, pp.117-8).

11. Because some increases in the Canadian production and export of arms will be connected to the US Strategic Defence Initiative (SDI) and the latter is seriously defective technologically, militarily and politically, we should at least resist any increases with such

23

connections (Tsipis 1986, pp.37-46; Sivard 1986, p.18). Tsipis concluded his review of SDI with the pronouncement that it is "voodoo science", and according to Nadis (1988, p.23), "In October of 1986, a poll found that 98 percent of the members of the [US] National Academy of Sciences in fields most relevant to SDI research believed that SDI could not provide an effective defense of the U.S. civilian population."

12. Because Canada is a relatively small country with a relatively small military establishment and presence in the world, we have the opportunity to initiate changes in our defence policies without creating significant shocks or threats to other countries. New Zealand has denied nuclear armed American warships the right to enter its ports and has established Nuclear-Weapons-Free Zones (NWFZs) covering over 65% of its population. Anderton (1986, p.193) suggested that a basic premise of such actions is simply that "... small nations must take a stand for peace themselves, if they hope to influence big nations." Thus, Canada might undertake a gradual phasing out of all arms manufacturing that is not directly connected to the particular needs of our own defence policies, assuming that the latter may be specified relatively independently of the policies of the American establishment. As of August 1987, there were over 166 NWFZs in Canada, including the cities of Toronto, Vancouver, Hamilton and Regina, and the provinces of Manitoba, Ontario and the Northwest Territories (Davies and Marchant 1986, p.239; Gaundun 1987, p.11). The New Democratic Party has proposed that Canada join its Nordic neighbours (Norway, Denmark, Sweden, Finland, Greenland and Iceland) in declaring all our countries a NWFZ, which would be

an important building-block for an Arctic common security system (New Democratic Party of Canada 1988, pp.35-6).

The United Nations report on Unilateral Nuclear Disarmament Measures (1985, p.1) argued for a gradual reduction in arms patterned after the historical trend of gradual increases. Thus, the "de-escalation and reversal" of the arms race "could be facilitated by unilateral initiatives of States aimed at reducing the level of international tension, gradually creating an atmosphere of mutual trust and confidence and in general improving the environment for negotiations on arms limitation and disarmament. ... the scope of unilateral initiatives... could include reductions in military expenditures, reductions in the number of troops, cuts in the number of certain types of weapons or even their elimination, moratoria and freezes, policies of no-first-use of nuclear weapons, establishment of nuclear-weapon-free zones and a wide variety of restraints in military programmes."

13. The biggest threats to international security in the future are scarcities of raw materials, environmental degradation, declining economic growth and the severely unequal distribution of the world's wealth. Since increases in the production and export of arms contributes nothing and even decreases resources available to address these problems, in the interest of increasing international security, we ought to reduce expenditures on the former in favour of expenditures on the larger threats (Sanger 1982, p.29; United Nations, Panel 1986, pp.2-4; Creighton 1987, p.5. Several attempts to construct broader, basically non-militaristic and globally realistic views about the nature of international security may be found in the United Nations, Department for Disarmament Affairs (1987)).

25

14. Because the need for arms is largely in the eye of the beholder, one ought to be skeptical about any alleged need calling for increases in the production and export of arms. Treddenick (1987, pp.15-8) gives about ten reasons for defence spending tending to become a bottomless pit, but the following remarks seem to capture a main source of the problem:

"As an economic good satisfying human wants, defence, at least in peacetime, is an abstract concept, one which is technically complex and generally not well understood by the public. It cannot be measured in any objective sense. Whether defence is adequately provided for, or whether the composition of defence spending, including the equipment mix, is appropriate is a matter of perceptions about intentions and relative force sizes, training, tactics, morale and so on. It is therefore impossible to say that there is too much or too little defence spending, or to say that there are too many tanks or too many ships in the same way that it is possible to say that there is too much of other types of goods. The relationship between spending on defence, including how it is spent, and how much defence capability is actually achieved is therefore highly ambiguous. This ambiguity can make defence planning a challenging occupation, but at the same time it provides economic policy makers with an expenditure instrument of a flexibility unmatched by other forms of government expenditure." Adeniji (1987, pp.103-4) takes a similar line.

15. There is some evidence from a national opinion poll taken in October 1987 that most Canadians would prefer to see less emphasis on a militaristic approach to international security, which would imply less emphasis on the production and export of arms. The survey was sponsored by the North-South Institute in Ottawa, and

the sponsors' analysts summarized their view of their findings as follows:

"The Canadian public seems to be on a completely different wavelength from its government in what it sees as the main threats to Canadian security and what should be done about them. In 1987 the government allowed a Defence White Paper to be seen to speak for Canadian security policy, and the Department of National Defence to be seen to shape Canada's views on peace and war. In the year that ended with Mr. Gorbachev in Washington signing the INF Treaty [banning missiles of intermediate range from Europe], NSI's [the North-South Institute's] survey shows most Canadians implicitly rejecting both the Cold War diagnoses and prescriptions of the Defence White Paper tabled by Mr Beatty [who was then Minister of National Defence] in June.

"Canadians themselves have a different and much wider agenda for enhancing international security, including environmental, health, developmental and ethical/political goals. In the maintenance of peace, they seem likely to see Canada's best contribution in more arms control and disarmament efforts, international cooperation, conflict resolution and peacekeeping, rather than in the build-up of arms. Even among various international purposes — quite apart from needs at home — most Canadians resoundingly reject increased defence spending as a priority." (North-South Institute 1988, p.2).

Regarding the last quoted sentence, given the survey question "If one wanted to increase Canada's influence internationally, which do you think would be most effective?", 6.2% answered "Increase the size of our armed forces", 10.4% said "spend more on aid for developing countries", 31.5% said "We should speak

27

out more often on international issues", and 48.7% said "Put more emphasis on our economic and trade power". Given the question "If the Canadian government had an additional sum of money to spend for international activities next year, which of the following options would you choose?", 5.0% said "Expand services at Canadian embassies and consulates abroad", 18.8% favoured "More equipment and personnel for Canada's national defence", 28.7% favoured "Expanded aid programs to Third World countries", and 44.4% wanted "Programs to increase our overseas trade". (North-South Institute 1988, pp.4, 12).

According to Lambert (1987, p.24), "Polls by Angus Reid and Goldfarb ... show the majority of Canadians opposed to cruise testing, opposed to the purchase of nuclear submarines, and in favor of making Canada a nuclear weapons free zone."

VI

Arguments for Producing and Exporting Arms

In this Section I review arguments that may be offered by Canadians in favour of the production and export of military arms, and I try to show that every one of them is defective.

1. Since sovereign nations have a right to defend themselves, they must have the right to purchase arms. The latter is plainly useless unless someone, at least some nation, has the right to produce and sell arms. There is no good reason to suppose that only this or that particular nation has a right to produce and sell arms. Thus, Canada or any other sovereign nation apparently has the right to produce and sell arms (Regehr 1987, p.xv. To avoid confusion, it may be worthwhile to point out that Regehr is a staunch opponent of militarism but he has provided an excellent review of many of the arguments for both sides of the issue).

Reply. Even if it is granted that in principle any nation has the right to produce and sell arms, it does not follow that in fact it is wise or morally right for every nation to engage in such activities. Presumably, the argument presupposes an 'if all other things are roughly equal' caveat. Without such a caveat, the argument might be used to justify the production and export of arms even in situations in which such activities prevented the production of such necessities as food and shelter. As already explained, there are many situations in which just such trade-offs are made and the existence of these cases shows the inherent limitations of the rights argument.

2. Since governments in particular have a responsibility to protect their territories and citizens, they must have a responsibility to provide arms as required for this task. Such a responsibility might be impossible to fulfill without military arms. Thus, governments must have the right to purchase arms, which again implies the right of someone to produce and sell them (Regehr 1987, p.xv).

Reply. The reply to the previous argument is applicable to this one too.

3. As a member of the sixteen-nation North Atlantic Treaty Organization (NATO), Canada has an obligation to 'contribute its fair share to the common defence'. Its contribution might be made by purchasing, producing, selling arms or any combination of these three, and Canada apparently has a right to fulfill its obligations to the alliance in any of these three ways (Canada, Department of National Defence 1987, pp.5-7; Regehr 1987, p.xvi).

Reply. Granting that Canada has a right to fulfill its obligations in any of these three ways, one might argue that the production and export of arms ought to be abandoned in favour of meeting our obligations only by purchasing arms from others. One might be led to this conclusion as a result of being persuaded by the positive arguments presented above against the production and export of arms. Since the adoption of this policy would increase the costs of arms procurement in several ways, it might lead to an overall reduction in military hardware which would also be an attractive consequence for people taking this line. I think the costs of adopting this approach to meeting our obligations to the NATO alliance would outweigh the benefits. We would become even more dependent on the United States than we are now, with all of the problems such dependency entails.

In my view, the appropriate response to this NATO obligations argument is withdrawal from the alliance. A thorough defence of this view would require a lengthy discussion, which would be out of place here. Briefly, however, I think that this alliance, like the seven-nation Warsaw Treaty, is an anachronism. For Canada NATO is a very expensive anachronism, since it carries a price-tag of over a billion dollars a year to keep our one brigade in Europe. As the New Democratic Party's Defence Critic (Blackburn 1987, p.6) wrote in response to the Tories' Defence White Paper: "It is simply expensive symbolism." Even if we stay in NATO, there is no good reason to maintain this expense.

The alliances may have made sense in the 1950s, but they have increasingly become part of the problem of international insecurity rather than part of the solution. The policies of each alliance are dominated by the biased views of the USA and the USSR, views that are effectively sensitive to East-West problems as defined by the superpowers and relatively blind to North-South problems as defined by the other 136 or so non-aligned nations on earth (Regehr 1987, p.186, 195-9). According to Sivard (1986, p.9), the USA and the USSR "have less than 11 percent of the world population but in 1985 they accounted for 23 percent of the world's armed forces, 60 percent of the military expenditures, more than 80 percent of the weapons research, and 97 percent of all nuclear warheads and bombs. ... Distrust between the two countries has been fanned by exaggerated fantasies on both sides and by careless rhetoric of political and military leaders."

There is no evidence that Canada has had and will have more influence on the United States inside than it

31

would have outside NATO, but it is certainly the case that Canada's membership in the alliance adds legitimacy to United States' policies pursued through the alliance. Virtually every arms-escalating defence initiative Canada has entertained in the past twenty years, if not longer, has been justified by our alleged obligations to NATO, e.g., renewing the North American Aerospace Defence Agreement (NORAD), deploying and increasing the number of Canadian troops and military hardware in Europe, testing cruise missiles over Alberta, allowing low-level flights of bombers over Labrador, having B-52 flight training over British Columbia, Alberta and Ontario, the preposterous proposal of purchasing nuclear submarines (to participate in the United States Navy's Forward Maritime Strategy) and allowing Canadian companies to participate in Star Wars research. Thus, in the interest of freeing Canada from its obligations to an anachronistic and dangerously biased alliance, and of strengthening such multilateral organizations as the United nations, we ought to withdraw from NATO. (The current Federal government, like the one before it, is committed to the alliance, as is clear from Canada, Department of National Defence 1987. For brief, but devastating critiques of the latter document, see Creighton 1987, pp.4-6; Epstein 1987, pp.6-7; Robinson 1987, p.9 and 1987a, pp.10-3).

4. Because we have a right to fulfill our obligations of alliances by producing and selling arms, and it is profitable to do so, it is prudent to do so (Regehr 1987, p.xvi). In the words of our Department of National Defence (1987, p.84), "Canadian defence spending contributes significantly to the maintenance of a robust and flexible economic environment. Defence purchases contribute to the development of internationally competitive Canadian industries."

Reply. For reasons already given and others yet to be presented, it cannot be granted that it is profitable and prudent to produce and sell arms, all things considered. However, even if it were granted, as in other classical cases of prisoners' dilemmas and the "tragedy of the commons", actions that are apparently reasonable from an individual's point of view narrowly construed may turn out to be disastrous given similar actions by many other individuals. Regehr (1987, p.10) pointed out that the result of such prudential reasoning is "an international arms trade that is out of control and serves as the pre-eminent vehicle for the militarization of the planet." What is worse, of course, is the fact mentioned above, namely, that the arms have been used to kill over 20 million people. Furthermore, "the intermingling of military and economic considerations may blunt the nation's sensitivity to the arms race with the result that incentives to search for ways to reduce armament expenditures may be submerged." (Treddenick 1985, p.91). The latter consideration is obviously applicable to all of the economic arguments for increases in the production and export of arms.

5. Since the production and export of arms to members of the NATO alliance allows us to increase standardization and create valuable economies of scale, it should be encouraged (Regehr 1987, p.8).

Reply. The reduction of the cost of producing anything that is morally, legally and rationally acceptable is generally laudable. However, as indicated in the previous Section, there are good reasons for thinking that increases in the production and export of arms are not morally or rationally acceptable.

6. Because the Canadian production and export of arms is such a small percentage of the world's total, it is relatively insignificant to particular recipients and to the

general world supply of arms. Besides, as indicated above in Section 4, the share of Canada's own economy devoted to armaments is also very small. So, nationally and internationally it has relatively little economic, moral or political significance (Regehr 1987, p.xvi).

Reply. Regarding the international aspect of this argument, Regehr (1987, p.20) responded as follows. "Canada's share of annual arms sales to the Third World is about 1 per cent. Since 1945 arms transfers have provided the fuel for more than 100 wars in the Third World, producing more than 20 million military and civilian combat deaths. One per cent of those deaths amounts to 200,000 — about twice the number of Canadians who have lost their lives as the result of war during this century." Assuming that non-Canadian lives are worth as much as Canadian lives, and that an economically, morally and politically significant number of the latter were lost in wars, it must be granted that the estimated 200,000 lives lost in Third World wars are also significant.

Regarding the national aspect of the argument, suppose that Treddenick's estimates are accurate and about half of 1% of the Canadian GNP is involved in arms production. In 1986 that would have been half of 1% of at least $500 billion or roughly $2.5 billion dollars. Two and a half billion dollars that year would have matched the Federal government's expenditures for Family Allowances and for Research and Development (R & D) in the natural sciences. It would have been 6 times the Federal government's expenditure on the environment, 13 times the expenditure for R & D in the social sciences and 3 times the expenditure on recreation and leisure. It would have just about matched the country's expenses on community colleges, and it would have added another 22,676 new or renovated housing units to the 56,689 units funded by the Federal government in 1986 (Statistics Canada, Federal Government Finances 1985 (68-211) pp.41-2; Canada Year Book 1988, 4-5, 7-5, 12-11). Clearly, since it would be unreasonable to dismiss all these national expenditures as economically, morally and politically insignificant, it must be granted that the sixth argument is unsound.

7. The greater a nation's military strength, the greater its influence in negotiations with other nations. Since the production and sale of new arms strengthens Canada, it also increases our ability to influence other nations in the removal of all arms (Regehr 1987, p.xviii).

Reply. It seems unlikely that Canada's military strength and influence based on it could be significantly increased without increasing defence expenditures beyond a point that would be acceptable even to most Canadian Cold Warriors. The people who are inclined to favour increases in our military strength tend to be the same people who favour keeping us in NATO, where we would always be dominated by the USA and the UK. While increases in military strength are apparently not sufficient to guarantee greater influence internationally, such increases are probably not even necessary. Even relatively small and militarily weak countries are able to have significant impacts in the various international organizations of the United Nations system, and the latter in turn have significant impacts on the so-called superpowers. Although one could always haggle about the meaning of 'significant impacts' and 'influence' in this context, I think those who would argue that the various organizations in the United Nations system (e.g., the World Health Organization, International Labour Office, UNESCO, etc.) are uniformly insignificant or powerless would find the historical record overwhelmingly against them.

8. The more arms a nation has, the less likely it is that they will be used. Since the production and sale of arms is a necessary condition of nations having arms, the former contributes to global stability and peace (Canada, Department of National Defence, 1987, p.5; Regehr 1987, p.xviii).

Reply. This argument is based on the Roman dictum which says "If you would have peace, prepare for war." It seems to have led and to lead directly to increases in the production and export of arms around the world, and consequently, to a highly insecure system of international security (Carroll 1986, pp.30-2; Robinson 1987, p.13; Adamichin 1987, pp.46-7; Cassese 1987, pp.144-5; Corradini 1987, pp.151-4; Sanger 1982, pp.28, 33). According to Sivard (1986, p.14), as the weapons of the USA and the USSR become more sophisticated, "The incentive grows to be the first to use the weapons, to destroy as much as possible of the enemy's nuclear forces before they can be fired. The chances of miscalculation, the fragility of 'deterrence', increase in proportion to the rise in numbers and the advance in technology."

Although increases in the numbers of nuclear weapons have not led to a nuclear war, there is a correlation between increases in the numbers of conventional weapons in Third World countries and wars (Regehr 1975, p.2). There are also many hypothetical scenarios leading from conventional wars to a nuclear war, e.g., in Greene, Percival and Ridge 1985, pp.17-22. Thus, in the interests of creating a more secure system of international security and reducing the numbers of wars in

Third World countries, increases in the production and export of arms should be resisted (Werlin 1986, p.94).

9. The production and export of arms should be encouraged because it will improve Canada's balance of payments, e.g., especially with regard to the 1963 DPSA with the USA and with the repatriation of petro-dollars (Regehr 1987, p.8).

Reply. Since Canada and the United States agreed to have a rough balance of arms trade through the DPSA, it is impossible for us to have a significant "balance of payment surplus or a net gain in jobs" in the long run in this area. Roughly speaking, every dollar spent in Canada by the United States must be matched by a dollar spent in the United States by Canada. So, there should be no balance of payments advantage in arms trade with our biggest trading partner. In spite of DPSA, Werlin (1986, p.99) claimed that "arms spending in Canada is a major factor contributing to our trade deficit in manufactured goods." Watkins claimed that when American subsidiaries in Canada sell arms to the United States, part of the former's profits are given back to their American parent firms and "there's no question that there's a net drain on the balance of payments that results from that." Besides, he claimed that because "foreign subsidiaries in Canada have a much higher tendency to import machinery and parts than do domestic, Canadian firms", that also has a negative effect on our balance of payments (Watkins in Discussion 1984, p.16).

10. The production and export of arms should be encouraged because it will create employment (Canada, Department of National Defence 1987, pp.83-4; Regehr 1987, p.8).

Reply. Our reply to this argument was already suggested in our reply to argument #9. Regehr (1987, p.175) says that "If military exports must, in the long run, be matched by military imports, then for every job that is created through exports, another job is lost by virtue of the reciprocal imports. Because a major part of Canada's capital defence budget is not spent in this country, Canadian military spending creates jobs in the United States, and to some extent in Europe, but not in Canada." Secondly, since investments in the arms industry typically produce fewer jobs per dollar than investments in most other industries (Table 5), any new government investments in job creation ought to give priority to the latter over the arms industry (Regehr 1987, pp.162-3, 169-70).

Furthermore, as Sanger (1982 p.40) explained, "military activities can be regarded as contributing to structural unemployment. [Because] ... military procurement crowds out capital investment in key civilian sectors, ... The countries which take on the heaviest burden of military expenditure tend to suffer a progressive decline in their international competitiveness as traders in civilian goods. They lose export markets, and even some of their domestic production is displaced by imports. Thus, a large military establishment begins to undermine the capacity of a country's economy to generate new employment over the long term." Hence, in the interest of increasing our capacity to create new jobs in Canada, we should withdraw from the DPSA and shift our investments to peaceful Canadian enterprises with relatively strong job creation possibilities. Additional references and arguments concerning the relatively limited job creation capacity of arms production may be found in Treddenick (1986) pp.34-5 and Melman (1984) p.5.

38

Table 5

Jobs Created by Spending One Billion Dollars
(1983 dollars)

1983-4 DND spending	22,000
Road and highway construction	37,000
Residential construction	38,000
Consumer spending	39,000
Hospital services	51,000
Education and related services	54,000
Radio and TV broadcasting	55,000
Urban transit systems	87,000
Post Office	90,000

Source:

T.Sanger, 'Military Spending', The Facts vol.8, No.1 (Canadian Union of Public Employees, Ottawa, January-February 1986).

11. The production of arms should be encouraged because it will generate technological spin-offs leading to increases in productivity (Regehr 1987, pp.8, 26).

Reply. On the contrary, increases in the production and export of arms ought to be resisted in Canada because they would retard commercial industrial innovation and civilian productivity. "Through an analysis of seventeen noncommunist industrialized countries over a period of two decades, the U.S. Council on Economic Priorities confirmed the observation that superior technological and industrial developments take place when the focus is on production for civilian use. Those economies with less emphasis on military production experienced faster growth and had a better job creation record." (Regehr 1987, p.165).

Figure 2 illustrates the inverse relationship between military expenditures as a percent of GNP and annual rates of manufacturing productivity growth for ten countries. Sivard (1986, p.20) wrote that "Since 1977, when WMSE [World Military and Social Expenditures] first illustrated this negative correlation, the pattern has not changed. Among major industrial countries, the highest rates of military expenditures are associated with low growth in productivity, as in USSR, US, and UK. In contrast, Japan with a very low military burden, has a good investment record, an exceptional 9 percent average gain in productivity, low unemployment, and a highly favorable competitive position in international markets — the very goals that debtors are searching for."

Sanger (1982, pp.37, 48-52) also cited evidence produced for the Thorsson Group showing that "military expenditure had a 'very negative effect' on the gross formation of private fixed capital and an indirectly negative influence on economic growth." As more research

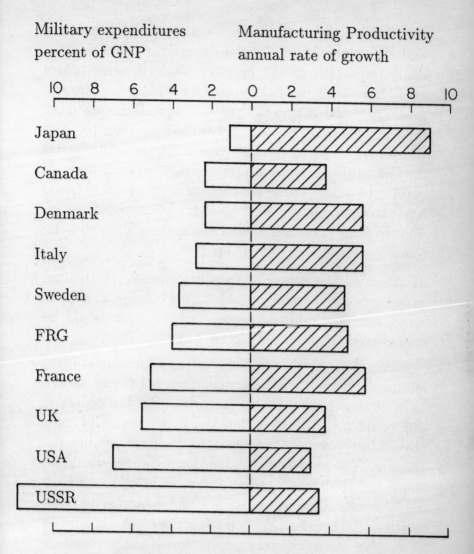

Military expenditures percent of GNP

Manufacturing Productivity annual rate of growth

Fig.2   Military burden and productivity, 1960-84

Source:

R.L. Sivard, <u>World Military and Social Expenditures 1986</u> (World Priorities Inc. Box 25140, Washington D.C., 20007) p 20, chart 11.

and development funds are poured into the aerospace and electronics sectors of the economy, which are especially important to the military establishment, "older basic industries, such as steel, automobiles, railroads, machinery and metal-working, are suffering from technological stagnation. This in turn causes lower productivity and a loss of competitiveness in those industries ... The situation is then often aggravated by a flight of capital to other countries, because investment at home has become unattractive." (Sanger 1982, p.39). A review of additional arguments along these lines may be found in Treddenick (1986) pp.23-9.

12. Because the export of arms helps to keep Canadian producers commercially viable and available as suppliers of our own military needs, such exports should be encouraged (Regehr 1987, pp.8, 51).

Reply. This argument is based on a questionable assumption, namely, that the manufacture of arms should be a commercially viable enterprise. On the contrary, one could take the view that the manufacture of arms should be a government sponsored, nonprofit, public enterprise. The only arms produced or exported would be those required by Canadian forces in their routine air and sea surveillance, patrolling and peacekeeping activities. As Regehr (1987, p.68) writes, "According to this assumption, military production is not a commercial activity like other commercial endeavours (just as prescription and other restricted drugs do not operate under usual market conditions). Thus, commercial viability is not a central question. This view of military production prevails in wartime, when military needs are defined without reference to economic opportunity or viability."

13. Insofar as the export of arms tends to lead to further exports of replacement parts, training and repair services, and some influence on the strategic planning and public policy-making of importing countries, such exports ought to be encouraged in order to strengthen Canada's international position (Regehr 1987, p.9).

Reply. This is an argument for the use of the same devious and dangerous influence-pedaling tactics employed by the world's major arms merchants. If Canada adopted such a policy, it would be yet another "clear case of the keepers of peace having turned freebooters" (Rasgotra 1987, p.136). Even if we ended up with a greater amount of international influence, it could serve no worthwhile purpose since we would have become part of the world's arms problem.

14. If Canada does not produce enough arms to appear as if it could defend itself or, minimally, as if it could provide adequate levels of surveillance for its northern borders, then the United States will probably become more active in the north. Since it is prudent to defend ourselves and our sovereignty against such increases of American activity around our northern borders, it is prudent to produce enough arms to perform this task. Producing arms for export, as indicated above, simply allows us to reduce the cost of such production (Regehr 1987, p.44).

Reply. This argument reveals Canada's precarious position regarding co-operation with the United States. It may be safely assumed that the Americans are going to be militarily active in the north for some years, with or without the co-operation of Canada. It may also be assumed that any perceived or actual lack of co-operation by Canada would create some friction and tension between the two countries, which both countries would like to avoid. Thus, the same assumptions that led us to accept the 1957 NORAD agreement giving the United States free access to Canadian airspace could lead us to a 'maritime NORAD' giving the Americans free access to our coastal waters, including the North-west Passage through our Arctic islands (Dyer 1988, p.4). In both cases co-operation implies a shared vision of a Soviet threat and an escalation of arms.

As one might expect given my view of NATO and NORAD, I think it is imperative that Canadians simply refuse to go along in order to get along with the American military establishment. We should not allow ourselves to be increasingly militarized in the interest of feeding American paranoia or an irrational "military-industrial complex". As Blackburn (1987, p.11) wrote, "We can contribute to stability and defence by putting in place surveillance, warning, and interception systems that would guarantee that no first-strike across Canadian territory could go undetected. The North American Aerospace Defence Agreement should be replaced with an agreement with the United States under which Canada would assume total responsibility for the conventional defence of its portion of the northern half of North America." Presumably, the last quoted sentence is simply a diplomatic way of telling one's neighbours to mind their own business. At the same time, we should initiate multilateral discussions in the United Nations with an aim to designing an international Arctic surveillance system that would give both the USA and the USSR guaranteed protection against any undetected first-strike operations.

15. Given the continuous development of sophisticated contemporary arms technology around the world, it is practically impossible for Canada to avoid relatively

44

permanent arms research and development without losing some competitive advantage. Thus, if we must have some arms research and development, we might as well try to offset its cost with exports (Regehr 1987, p.45).

Reply. This argument is based on the assumption that marginal technological improvements are militarily significant, which is unbelievable given the current levels of conventional and nuclear arms around the world. The argument also seems to assume that there could be something like a technological final solution which would guarantee military superiority to its inventor and which would justify continuing massive R & D expenditures in search of it. Again, this assumption is unwarranted for the same reason as the first. The technological arms race presupposed by this argument ended some years ago, and everybody lost. The great task before us now is to design political institutions that will make the world secure from a military disaster.

16. Caldicott (1986, p.312) presented the following argument as representative of the view of the US-based Committee on the Present Danger. "You can't trust the Russians because they cheat on treaties. If the Soviets cheat on treaties, you can't have arms control, and if you can't have arms control, nuclear war becomes inevitable. If nuclear war is inevitable, then America has to prepare to fight and win a nuclear war." For our purposes, one would add: If America has to prepare to fight and win a nuclear war, then so does Canada.

Reply. If we ignore the assumption that the Soviets are any less trustworthy than the Americans, the Committee's last premise is a non sequitur. If nuclear war is inevitable then so is nuclear winter, in which most of the people of the northern hemisphere will die (Caldicott 1986, pp.317-8; Greene, Percival and Ridge 1985). The

45

one great fact to be remembered about so-called nuclear war is that it is virtual suicide for people living in the northern hemisphere. For these people it may be assumed that there will be practically no winners or losers. It does not matter where the bombs go off first or who has more to explode. For these people there is an open question regarding what, if anything, they rationally or morally ought to do now. Quite apart from the prospect of nuclear war, we all know we are going to die sooner or later and that fact does not seem to imply any particular course of action. Different people cope with mortality in different ways. On the other hand, for those of us who do not believe that war is inevitable, it seems both reasonable and morally responsible to try to find ways to decrease its likelihood. Decreasing the production and export of arms is certainly one way.

If we ignore nuclear weapons and the possibility of a nuclear war, it is worthwhile to consider a war fought only with conventional weapons and the consequences of exploding nuclear reactors. Clearly, in any war between members of NATO and the Warsaw Pact, some nuclear reactors would be destroyed. Depending on how reactors were damaged, there would be relatively localized blow-ups, massive melt-downs and middle-sized messes. When the reactor at Chernobyl blew its top, agricultural land, people and animals were poisoned thousands of miles away in Sweden and the United Kingdom. No one knew exactly how much radioactive fallout would be produced by the explosion, how far the winds would carry it, in what direction and with what consequences in human casualties in the long and short run. There are about 370 operating nuclear reactors in the world now, most of which are in Europe and North America. In a war any of these might be damaged by a variety of means. In the past, people dropped bombs, killed 'enemies', negotiated peace with survivors and went home. But even if only conventional weapons were used in a war between East and West, the destruction of some of our vast numbers of nuclear reactors would guarantee that there would be deadly radioactive material carried by the winds, groundwater movements and other natural water cycles to millions of people in North America and Europe no matter where the explosions occur. The 'victors' might have no homes to go to. Even if one assumes that a war between East and West with only conventional weapons is inevitable, it does not follow that Canada ought to be increasing its production and export of arms. The predictable catastrophic consequences of such a war still leave an open question regarding what, if anything, one rationally or morally ought to do. On the other hand, the best course of action for the rest of us is still to try to decrease the likelihood of such a war by decreasing the production and export of arms.

VII

Conclusion

The UNESCO Charter reminds us that "Since wars begin in the minds of men, it is in the minds of men that the defence of peace must be constructed." I am enough of a feminist to believe that even if the original authors of that sentence understood the term 'men' in its generic sense, it has special reference to males. We are the ones typically socialized to be competitive, aggressive, out of touch with our feelings and all too often arrogantly defensive of our own ignorance. So, I hope that men especially will give serious consideration to this essay.

As I remarked at the beginning, insofar as my arguments are sound, a case should have been made for resisting the current Federal government's proposed increases in the production and export of arms, and for beginning to scale down Canada's current militaristic activities. I have not recommended total disarmament or the gradual phasing out of our military establishment. On the contrary, I have suggested that the latter has a legitimate role to play both nationally and internationally with such things as routine surveillance, disaster relief and peacekeeping. We need a defence policy based not on military might but on wisdom, compassion and diplomacy. As the New Democratic Party of Canada (1988, p.50) put it: "Canadian security depends upon a stable international order that recognizes and respects Canadian sovereignty and territory, rather than on Canada's ability to defend itself militarily. Thus, Canada's primary responsibility in its own defence is to contribute to the development of a just international order. The role of the United Nations is central to this process."

References

Adamichin, A.: 1987, Working session no.1, **Symposium on Global Security for the Twenty-First Century**, United Nations Department for Disarmament Affairs (New York, United Nations) pp.41-50.

Adeniji, O.: 1987, Working session no.3, **Symposium on Global Security for the Twenty-First Century**, United Nations Department for Disarmament Affairs (New York, United Nations) pp.99-112.

Anderton, J.P.: 1986, 'Nuclear freedom in one country — how and why: a case study of the development of a nuclear-free policy in New Zealand', **End the Arms Race: Fund Human Needs**, ed. by T.L. Perry and J.G. Foulks (West Vancouver, Gordon Soules Book Pub.) pp.185-95.

Blackburn, D.: 1987, **Canadian Sovereignty, Security and Defence: A New Democratic Response to the Defence White Paper**, (Ottawa, New Democratic Party).

Caldicott, H.: 1986, 'Commit yourself to saving the earth', **End the Arms Race: Fund Human Needs**, ed. by T.L. Perry and J.G. Foulks (West Vancouver, Gordon Soules Book Pub.) pp.311-20.

Canada, Department of National Defence: 1987, **Challenge and Commitment: A Defence Policy for Canada** (White Paper on Defence),(Ottawa, Minister of Supply and Services).

Carroll, E.J.: 1986, 'A new concept for security in the nuclear age', **End the Arms Race: Fund Human Needs**, ed. by T.L. Perry and J.G. Foulks (West Vancouver, Gordon Soules Book Pub.) pp.29-36.

Cassese, A.: 1987, Closing session, **Symposium on Global Security for the Twenty-First Century**, United Nations Department for Disarmament Affairs (New York, United Nations) pp.143-50.

Corradini, A.: 1987, 'The quest for real security', **Symposium on Global Security for the Twenty-First Century**, United Nations Department for Disarmament Affairs (New York, United Nations) pp.151-63.

Creighton, P.: 1987, **Cold war heat**, The Ploughshares Monitor, **8**, pp.4-6.

Davies, L. and G. Marchant: 1986, 'The special role of munici- palities in working for peace', **End the Arms Race: Fund Human Needs**, ed. by T.L. Perry and J.G. Foulks (West Vancouver, Gordon Soules Book Pub.) pp.235-44.

DeRoo, R.J.: 1986, 'Our war economy and conversion for peace', **End the Arms Race: Fund Human Needs**, ed. by T.L. Perry and J.G. Foulks (West Vancouver, Gordon Soules Book Pub.) pp.81-91.

Dyer, G.: 1988, **Nuclear submarines and our Canadian politics**, The Mercury, March 5, p.4.

El-Shafei, O.: 1987, Working session no.3, **Symposium on Global Security for the Twenty-First Century**, United Nations Department for Disarmament Affairs (New York, United Nations) pp.113-20.

Epps, K.: 1987, **More military work on Canadian campuses**, The Ploughshares Monitor, **8**, pp.8, 16.

Epps, K.: 1987a, **Canadian military industry update**, The Ploughshares Monitor, **8**, pp.10-2.

Epstein, W.: 1987, **Is Canada joining the arms race?**, The Ploughshares Monitor, **8**, pp.6-7.

Galbraith, J.K.: 1986, 'The military power: tension as a servant; arms control as an illusion', **End the**

Arms Race: Fund Human Needs, ed. by T.L. Perry and J.G. Foulks (West Vancouver, Gordon Soules Book Pub.) pp.103-10.

Garcia Robles, A.: 1987, Working session no.2, **Symposium on Global Security for the Twenty-First Century**, United Nations Department for Disarmament Affairs (New York, United Nations) pp.81-90.

Gaundun, K.: 1987, **NWFZ: the Canadian scene**, Peace Magazine, **3**, p.11.

Greene, O., I. Percival and I. Ridge: 1985, **Nuclear Winter: The Evidence and the Risks** (Cambridge: Polity Press).

Gumbleton, T.: 1986, 'The arms race protects the power and wealth of the privileged', **End the Arms Race: Fund Human Needs**, ed. by T.L. Perry and J.G. Foulks (West Vancouver, Gordon Soules Book Pub.) pp.129-36.

Kelly, P.: 1986, 'New forms of power: the Green Feminist view', **End the Arms Race: Fund Human Needs**, ed. by T.L. Perry and J.G. Foulks (West Vancouver, Gordon Soules Book Pub.) pp.207-25.

Lambert, S.: 1987, **The Canadian Peace Pledge Campaign**, Peace Magazine, **3**, p.24.

Melman, S.: 1984, **Peace, employment and the economics of permanent war**, Project Ploughshares Working Paper 84-5, pp.1-7.

Michalos, A.C.: 1980, North American Social Report, bf 1: **Foundations, Population and Health** (Dordrecht, D. Reidel Pub. Co.).

Michalos, A.C.: 1980a, North American Social Report, **2: Crime, Justice and Politics** (Dordrecht, D. Reidel Pub. Co.).

Michalos, A.C.: 1981, North American Social Report, **3: Science, Education and Recreation** (Dordrecht, D. Reidel Pub. Co.).

Michalos, A.C.: 1981a, North American Social Report, **4: Environment, Transportation and Housing** (Dordrecht, D. Reidel Pub. Co.).

Michalos, A.C.: 1982, North American Social Report, **5: Economics, Religion and Morality** (Dordrecht, D. Reidel Pub. Co.).

Miller, J.: 1986, 'The arms race and suffering in the Third World: one problem', **End the Arms Race: Fund Human Needs**, ed. by T.L. Perry and J.G. Foulks (West Vancouver, Gordon Soules Book Pub.) pp.125-27.

Nadis, S.: 1988, **After the boycott**, Science for the People, **20**, pp.21-6.

New Democratic Party of Canada: 1988, **Canada's Stake in Common Security** (Ottawa, New Democratic Party of Canada).

North-South Institute: 1988, **Fighting different wars: Canadians speak out on foreign policy**, Review '87/Outlook '88, pp.1-13.

Pentz, M.: 1986, 'To prevent nuclear war and promote nuclear disarmament: it's time for a new look', **End the Arms Race: Fund Human Needs**, ed. by T.L. Perry and J.G. Foulks (West Vancouver, Gordon Soules Book Pub.) pp.271-95.

Perry, T.L.: 1986, 'What the arms race is doing to people in the Third World', **End the Arms Race: Fund Human Needs**, ed. by T.L. Perry and J.G. Foulks (West Vancouver, Gordon Soules Book Pub.) pp.167-77.

Prince, M.J.: 1986, 'The Mulroney agenda: a right turn for Ottawa?', **How Ottawa Spends; 1986-87: Tracking the Tories**, ed. by M.J. Prince (Toronto, Methuen Pub.) pp.1-60.

Rasgotra, M.: 1987, Working session no.3, **Symposium on Global Security for the Twenty-First Century**, United Nations Department for Disarmament Affairs (New York, United Nations) pp.129-39.

Regehr, E.: 1975, **Making a Killing: Canada's Arms Industry** (Toronto, McClelland and Stewart Ltd.).

Regehr, E.: 1987, **Arms Canada: The Deadly Business of Military Exports** (Toronto, James Lorimer and Co.).

Robinson, B.: 1987, **Canada's White Paper doesn't add up**, The Ploughshares Monitor, **8**, p.9.

Robinson, B.: 1987, **Is NATO hopelessly outnumbered?**, The Ploughshares Monitor, **8**, pp.10-3.

Sanger, C.: 1982, **Safe and Sound: Disarmament and Development in the Eighties** (Ottawa, Deneau Pub.).

Sivard, R.L.: 1986, **World Military and Social Expenditures 1986** (Washington, World Priorities).

Sivard, R.L.: 1987, **World Military and Social Expenditures 1987-8** (Washington, World Priorities).

Statistics Canada: 1987, **Federal Government Finance 1985** (68-211) (Ottawa, Minister of Supply and Services).

Statistics Canada: 1987a, **Canada Year Book 1988** (Ottawa, Minister of Supply and Services).

Treddenick, J.M.: 1984, **The arms race and military Keynesianism**, Center for Studies in Defence

Resources Management, Report No.3, (Kingston, Royal Military College of Canada).

Treddenick, J.M.: 1985, **The arms race and military Keynesianism"** Canadian Public Policy - Analyse de Politiques, **11**, pp.77-91.

Treddenick, J.M.: 1986, **The military Keynesianism debate**, Center for Studies in Defence Resources Management, Report No.9, (Kingston, Royal Military College of Canada).

Treddenick, J.M.: 1987, **The economic significance of the Canadian defence industrial base**, Center for Studies in Defence Resources Management, Report No.15, (Kingston, Royal Military College of Canada).

Tsipis, K.: 1986, 'Technical and operational considerations of space-based defensive systems', **End the Arms Race: Fund Human Needs**, ed. by T.L. Perry and J.G. Foulks (West Vancouver, Gordon Soules Book Pub.) pp.37-46.

United Nations, Department for Disarmament Affairs: 1985, **Unilateral Nuclear Disarmament Measures** (New York, United Nations).

United Nations, Department for Disarmament Affairs: 1987, **Symposium on Global Security for the Twenty-First Century** (New York, United Nations).

United Nations, Panel of Eminent Personalities in the Field of Disarmament and Development: 1986, **Disarmament and Development** (New York, United Nations).

United Nations, Expert Group on the Relationship between Disarmament and Development: 1981, **Disarmament and Development** (The Thorsson Report), (New York, United Nations).

Wallace-Deering, K.: 1986, 'The economics of war and peace', **End the Arms Race: Fund Human Needs**, ed. by T.L. Perry and J.G. Foulks (West Vancouver, Gordon Soules Book Pub.) pp.75-80.

Watkins, M.: 1984, **Roundtable Discussion**, in Project Plough- shares Working Paper 84-5, pp.11-8.

Werlin, D.L.: 1986, 'Conversion to peaceful production', **End the Arms Race: Fund Human Needs**, ed. by T.L. Perry and J.G. Foulks (West Vancouver, Gordon Soules Book Pub.) pp.93-102.

Wilson, L.M.: 1986, 'Blessed are the peacemakers', **End the Arms Race: Fund Human Needs**, ed. by T.L. Perry and J.G. Foulks (West Vancouver, Gordon Soules Book Pub.) pp.137-45.

ABOUT THE AUTHOR

Alex Michalos has been a professor of philosophy and social sciences at the University of Guelph since 1966. He works in the field of social indicators and quality-of-life measurement, and has published 11 books, 50 articles and 160 reviews. He founded and is the editor of two scholarly journals, *Social Indicators Research* and the *Journal of Business Ethics*. In 1984 his 5 volume North American Social Report received the Secretary of State's award for excellence in interdisciplinary studies in the field of Canadian Studies.

Other books by Alex Michalos include *Principles of Logic* (Prentice-Hall, 1969), *Improving Your Reasoning* (Prentice-Hall, 1970), *The Popper/Carnap Controversy* (Martinus Nijhoff, 1971), and *Foundations of Decision-Making* (Canadian Library of Philosophy, 1978).